"I became a Buddhist because I hated my husband"

Pema Chodron

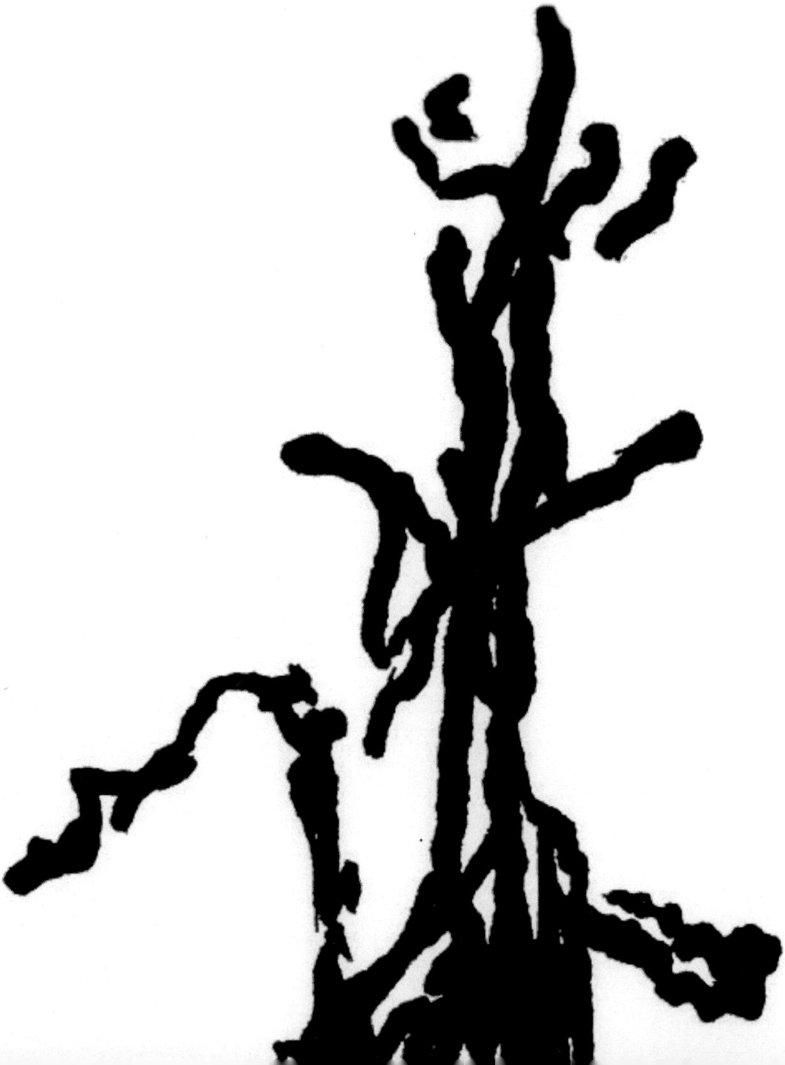

50 WAYS TO BLEED YOUR LOVER

Written by Rachel Dunphy

Supporting Author David Anthony Childs

living blueprint

FIRST EDITION

Paintings by Rachel Dunphy

All book artwork by Rachel Dunphy

Artwork modification by David Anthony Childs

Cover Design and book layout by David Anthony Childs

ISBN 978-1-7777854-0-6

50 Ways to Bleed Your Lover

RACHEL DUNPHY

supporting author

David Anthony Childs

for you, I'd bleed myself dry

We live in an abnormally aggressive world. Domestic abuse and even femicide (a word I had never heard until recently) has reached appalling heights.

I'm sharing this writing only to offer a knowing hug to your pain and understanding to your outrage. This macabre collection is shared with my highest intention to heal completely and help others do the same. It's my attempt at exposing our bad behaviours to the light, and more importantly, to share that the desire to lash out is a universal, understandable response to the cumulative damage that unethical actions of others can induce in us.

At 34, I lost my first born and only child. Then my partner of nearly a decade left me abruptly for someone else. That set off a chain of events that made me incapable of functioning for a few years. I was unemployed, addicted to oversleeping and substances, and worse still, unsupported and avoided by my community and the several institutions I reached out to.

There was somehow still something in me that asserted strongly,

"My story can't end like this."

Now, 17 years later, I am married to the love of my life on the West Coast of Canada. We care for two women in our owned home, along with two elderly, angel dogs, and are gifted with all the time in the world to pursue our hearts' desire which, for both of us, aligns with the Noble Path of Buddhism.

I can now truly let my past rest and even say, as horrible as it was, I would not change a thing because it got me to such a profound and lasting refuge of understanding. I know that this collective movement toward healing is only beginning and I feel so blessed to watch as the world continues to deepen in awareness and growing compassion.

I hope this book will reach into the darkest corners of those human hearts still hardened in defense from a broken world. The bigger picture truth is that we can and must heal our trauma which I believe we all have been subject to just by existing at this time, if only in our inherited patterns of unease, ignorance and delusion.

I am living proof that all good broken people of the world who hold their hearts open despite enormous odds, get to live as, and be surrounded by, real superheroes. And our numbers are finally, palpably growing. Our liberation toward right seeing and corrected understanding truly is the best vengeance of all.

These poems are all based on true events. Except, of course, for MOST of the violence

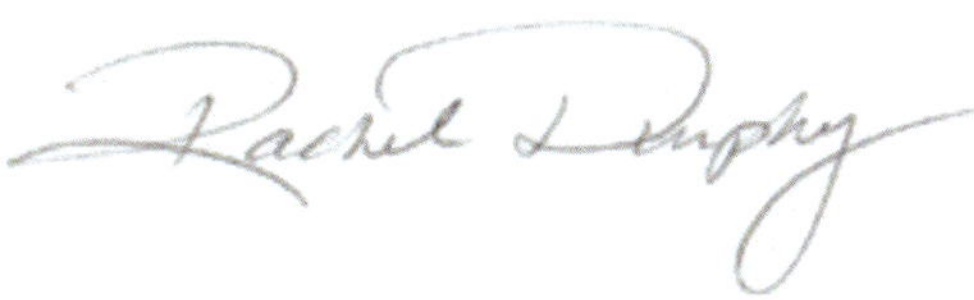

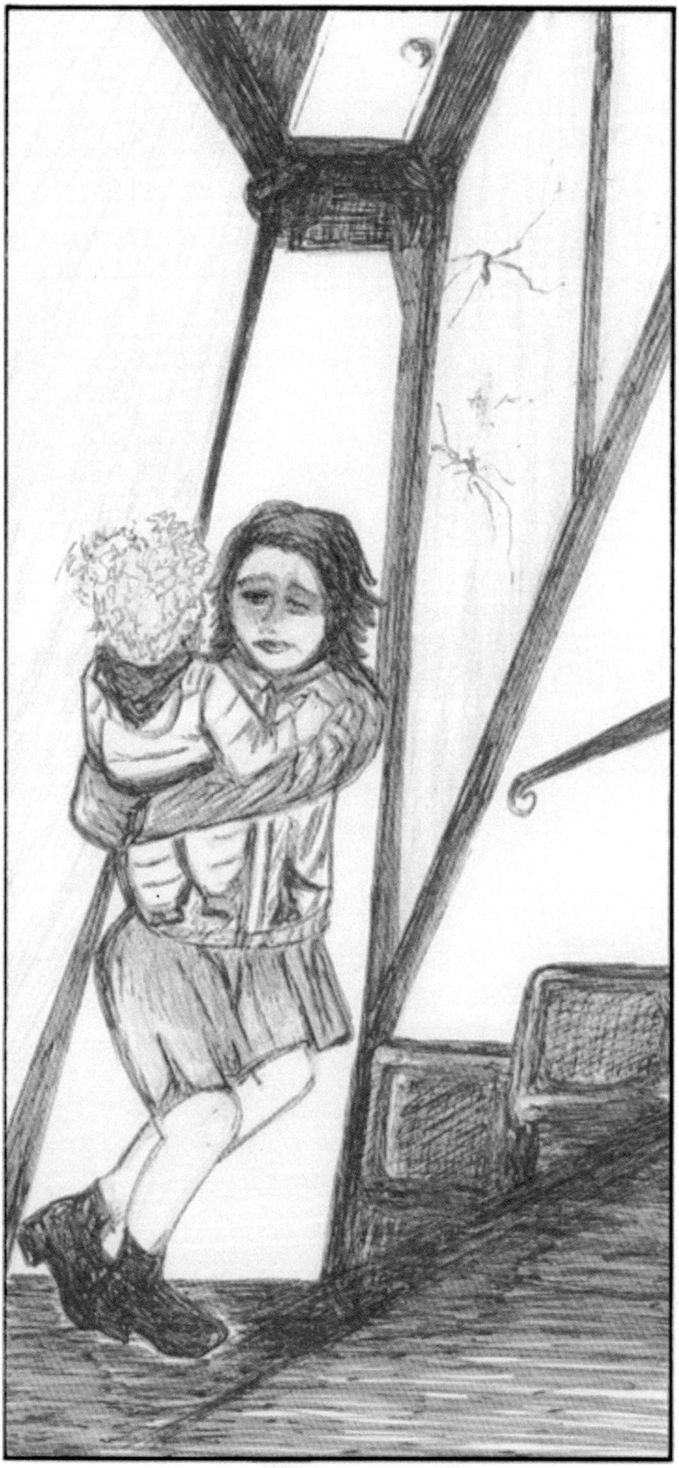

deepest of scars

Daddy liked to chase girls and race cars

At age 3 he made Mommy see stars

Screaming, "Daddy, don't hit!"

I just knew we would split

My first memory and deepest of scars

if a kid were a penny

"You're ugly," Sam hollered at school
I just shrank and I felt like a tool
Then a wrench struck his head
And no, he's not dead
But all he can do now is drool

Our gym teacher fondled so many
He'd be rich if each kid were a penny
Mr. B lost it all
But his brain can't recall
And his eyes have no light, no not any

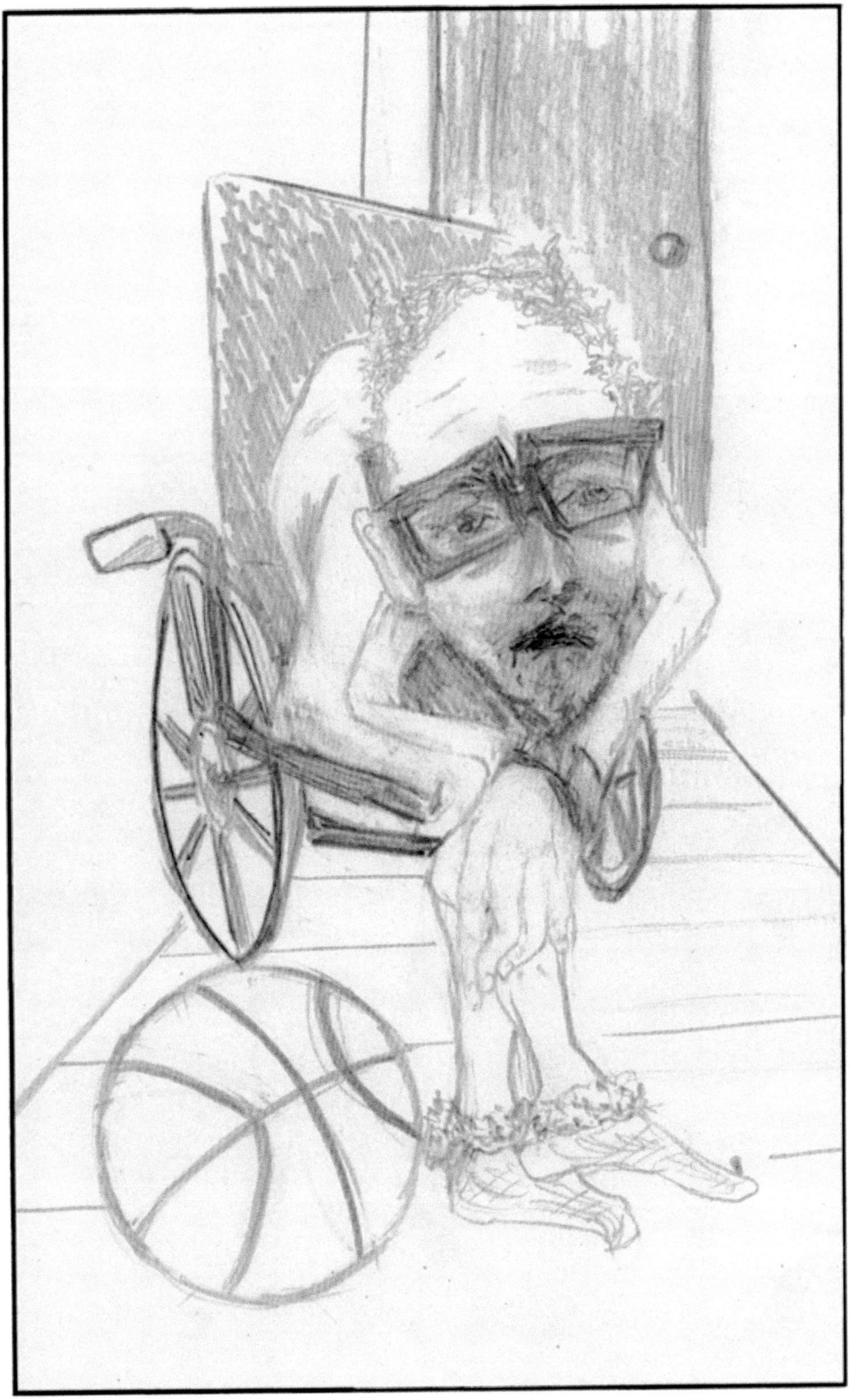

a bat & a fright

2 street kids I knew slept with men

Those kids were 11 and 10

What sick f#ck pays for that?!

Friends of mine found a bat

And those men won't f#ck children again

Tim was a tall handsome sleaze

He kept pushing me down to my knees

But he got quite a fright

When I took a big bite

I've heard his parts look like Swiss cheese

a blind eye

"I had sex with your friend", said her Dad

"It just happened," he said, "don't be mad"

Her friend was 15

She felt sick and obscene

They both fell from a cliff

Oh how sad

Our hockey team raped Adeline

She was sassy but friendly and kind

They said, "She didn't care"

But drunk "she" wasn't there

In time every last one would go blind

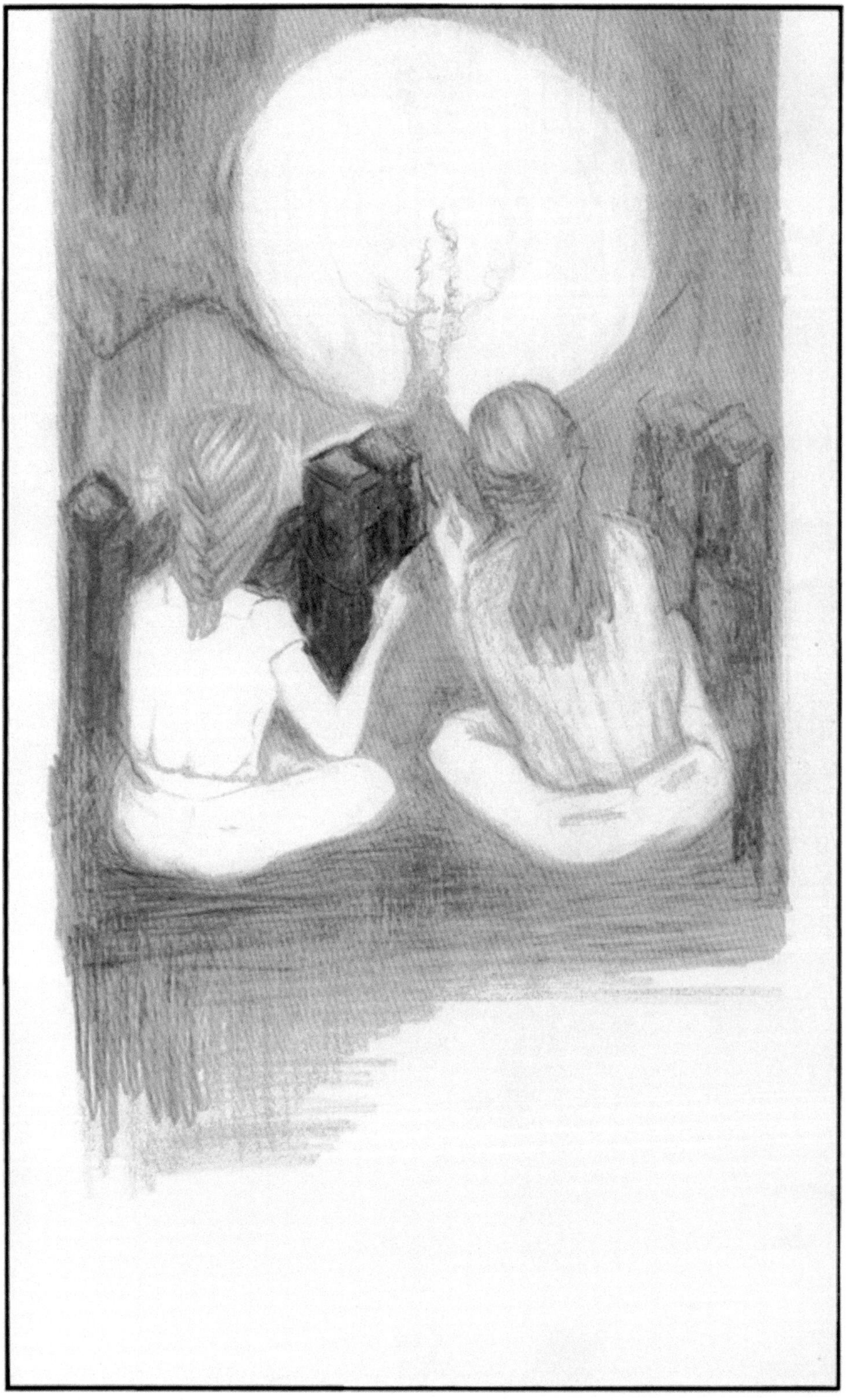

on the rocks

One night us girls partied with jocks

They drank and smoked down at the docks

It was not what we hoped

Us girls just got groped

They were pushed to their deaths on the rocks

good bye

Who leaves when a partner has cancer?

Well my darling, I'll offer my answer

Those who don't deserve breath

We'll just shrug at their death

One less pestilent, darkness enhancer

set free

Kent liked to wear a mohawk

And he stuffed his tight jeans with a sock

I caught him with a looker

Who 'turned out was a hooker

So I opened their heads with a rock

a clean slate

Shar and Cole were knocked-up at 16

As if that weren't enough of a scene

Shar found Cole in her bed

As her Mom gave him head

They were shot but her record's still clean

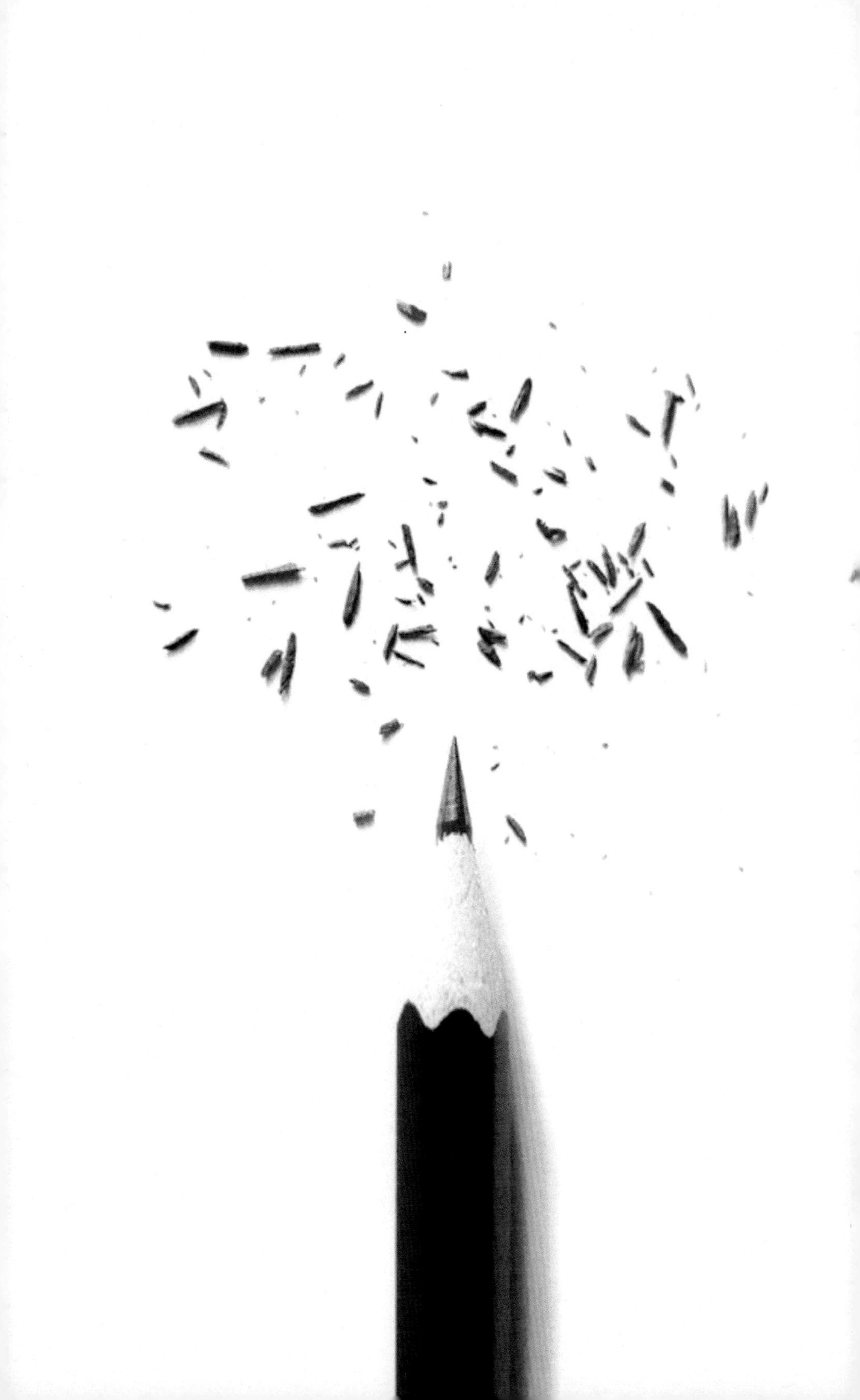

the lake

Robert brought SO much heartache

He just slipped in a girl "by mistake"

That man was a slut

And so he was cut

His

"manhood"

now

lies

in

a

lake

time for rest

The cops came for Reggie one day

The kids watched as they took him away

He had beaten some hoes

Broke their jaw and their nose

Deep down in the bog does he lay

innocent

Bob the slob stood me up for my prom

As hours went by I stayed calm

Then all cute in my gown

I hunted him down

He was stabbed to death on his front lawn

stone cold soup

Frank told me that he was all that

He got kicks out of saying "You're fat"

So I made a nice stew

Shot of arsenic or two

Now he's stiff as a board

How 'bout that?

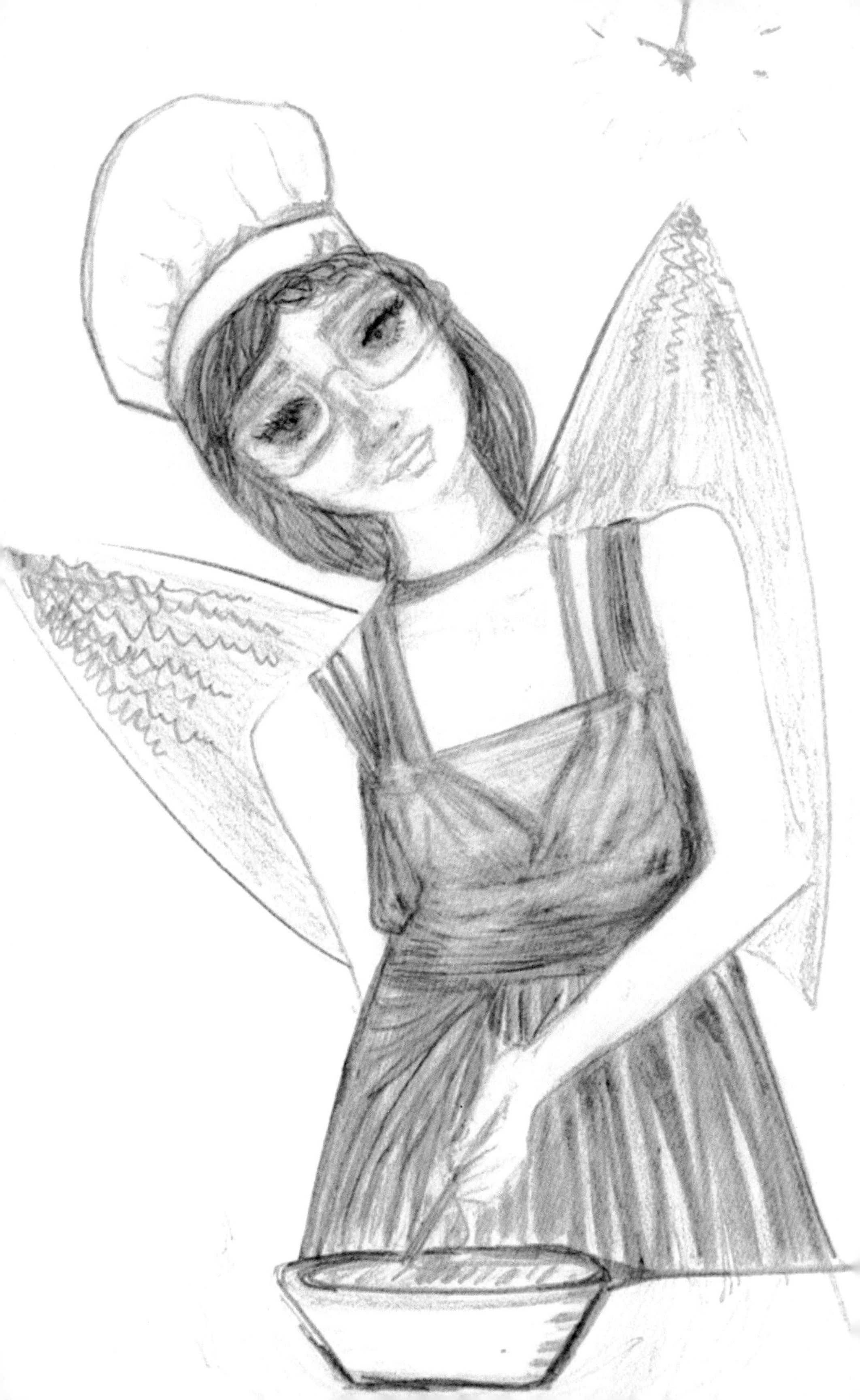

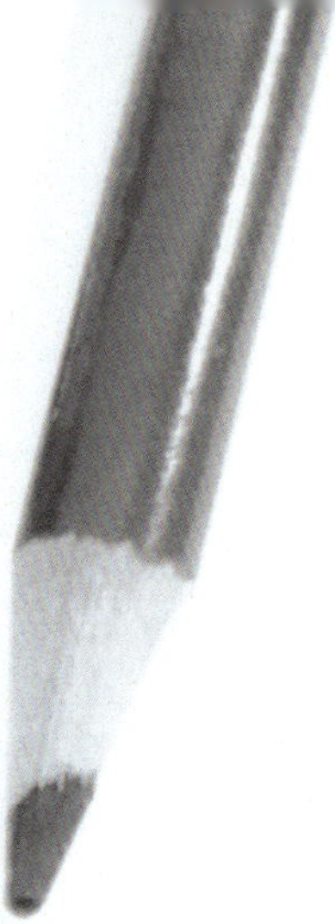

order up

Whatever happened to pedophile Ted

They say that he drank himself dead

Pretty wild, don't you think?

What can drop in a drink

So easy it boggles my head

besties

Paul "had to" have threesomes with me

If I didn't we just couldn't be

Jan and I made a plan

For revenge on that man

Arsenic was stirred into his tea

so limitless and free

Again Chris was with my best friend

I told him, "This time it's the end."

He begged and he cried

But our love had just died

The woodchipper made them a blend

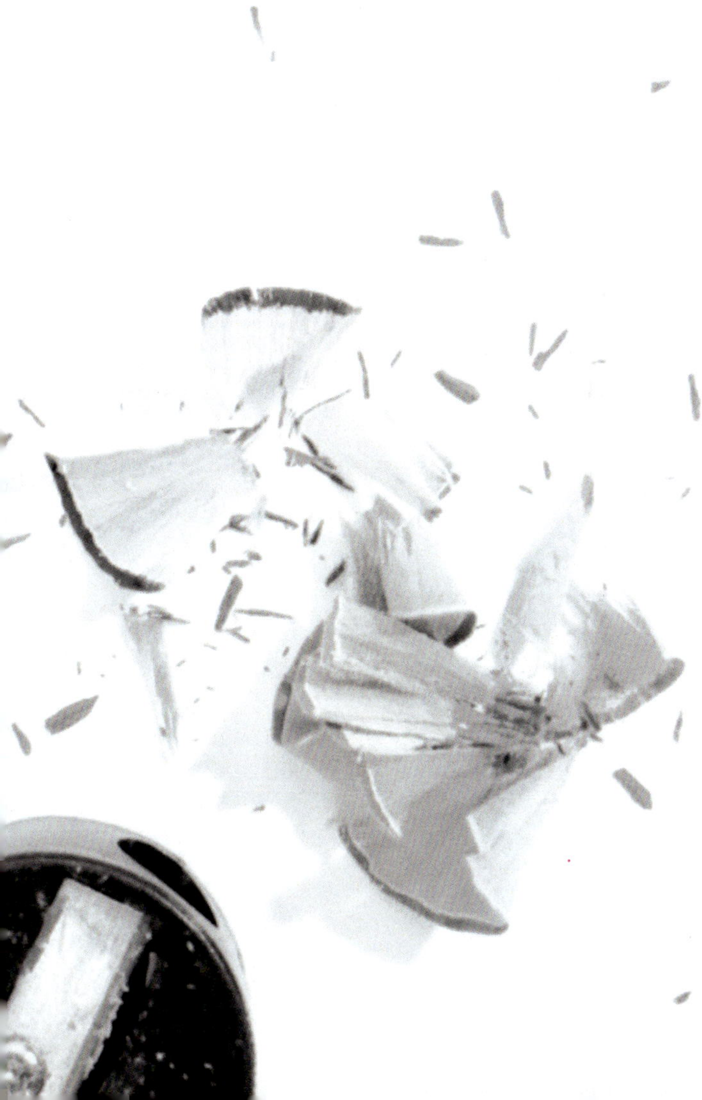

wings

Taylor was such a great lover

He liked to bite hard on my neck

And so suddenly

He had to be free

So I helped him fly off the back deck

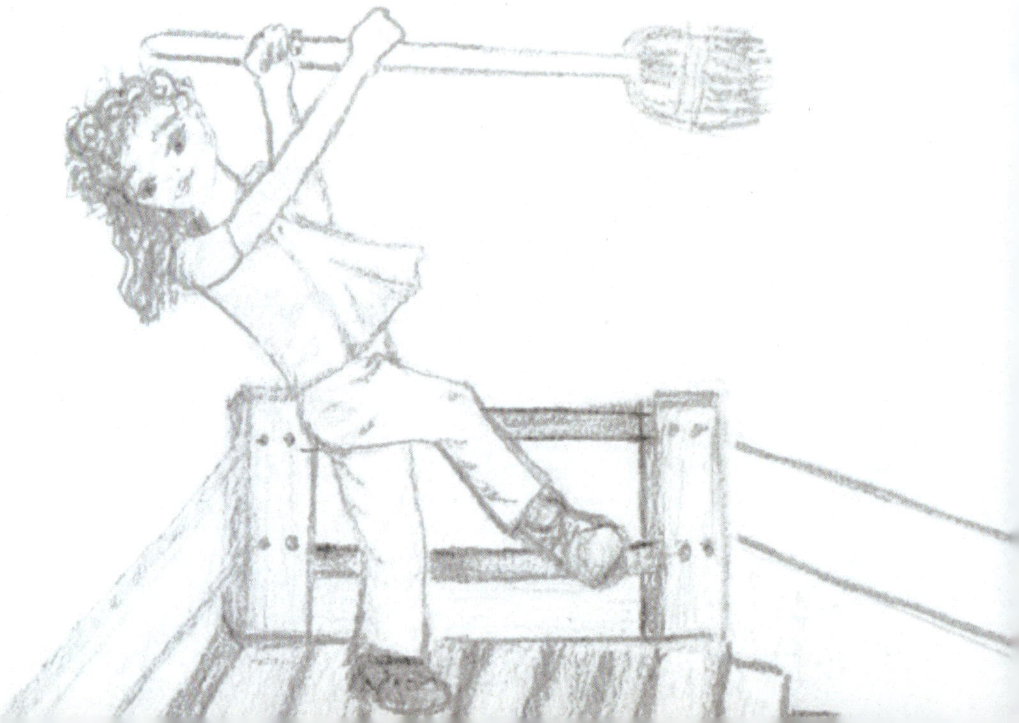

he's old

Stanley was lacking in passion
There just seemed to be no more flame
When he came home and said
"This relationship's dead"
He just slipped down the stairs, what a shame

and his skin is cold

Bradly seemed like an interesting guy
"Til the night he gave me a black eye
So my pit bull named Bill
Who I had trained to kill
Ate the side of his face and one thigh

the killer awoke

Clarence was touching her daughter

And a rage just consumed her to slaughter

So the three went out sailing

And watched his last flailing

'Til he cried and just went under water

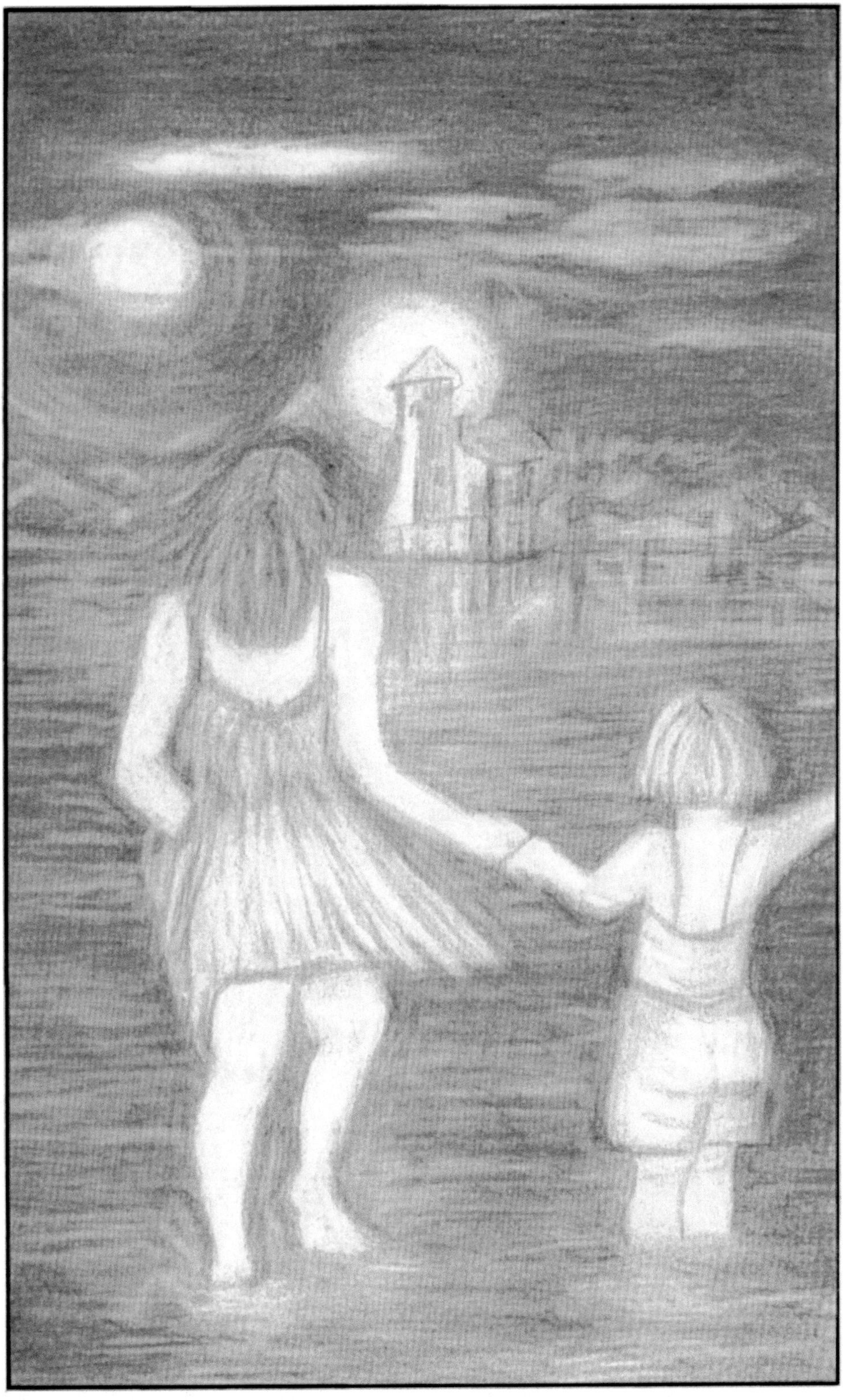

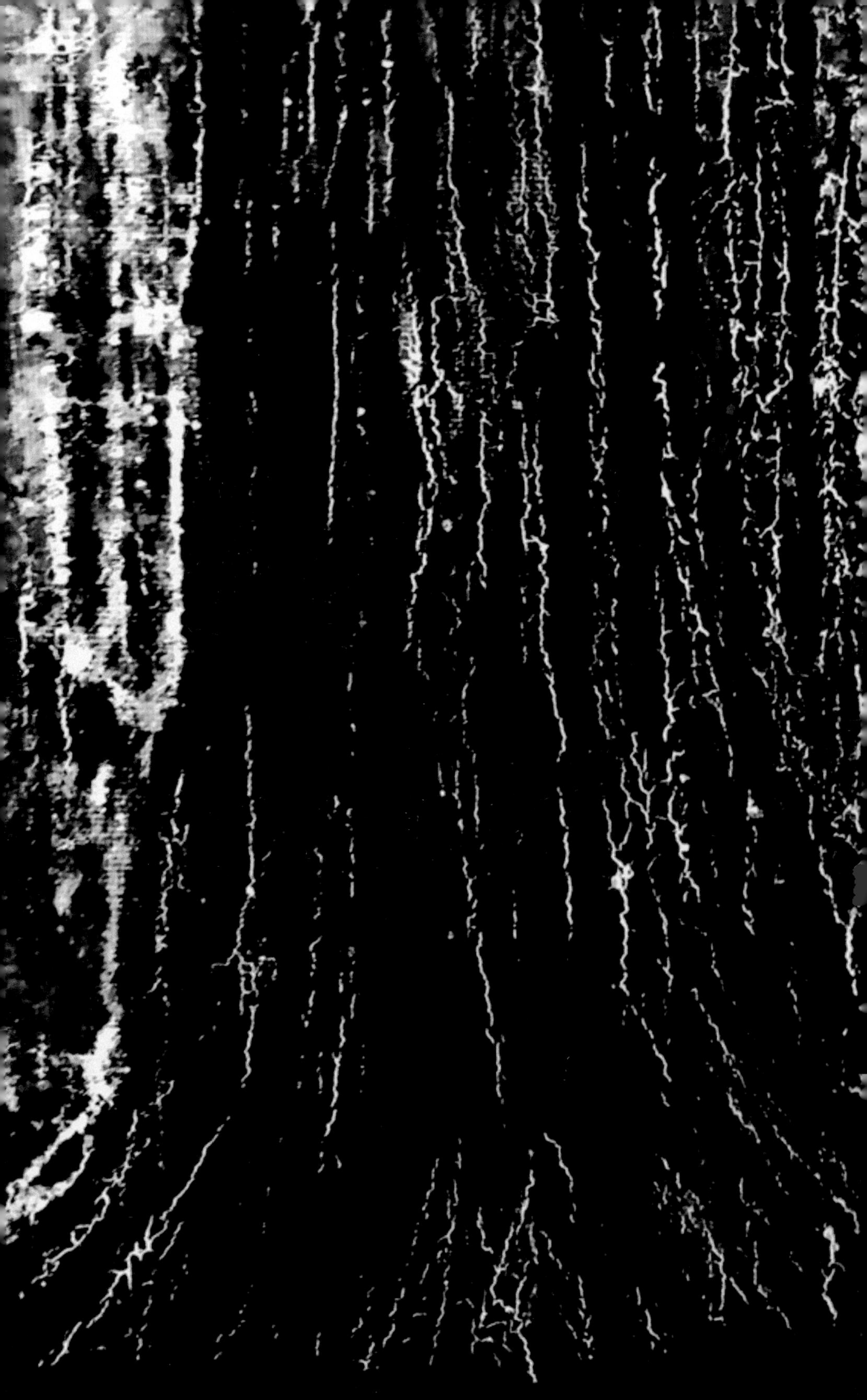

there's danger

Barry was one sassy dude

I liked him although he was rude

But he cheated on me

So I clubbed him at sea

And I smiled as the sharks ate their food

get here

Crazy Jack sold his daughter for drugs

She was 12 when he gave her to thugs

Jack sure had a fit

Tied outside with no hit

Now his bones are licked clean by the bugs

we'll do the rest

And along came that cute Yankee Chuck

"Our love", he said, made him "feel stuck"

When he cheated again

I stayed calm and quite Zen

Superglue in his condoms did suck

hunger

Robin the biker seemed cool

He often made all the girls drool

After sex he went cold

"It's just sex" I was told

"It's just death" I said, to the DEAD FOOL

a close call

Oh Randy we nearly got hitched

But you left me like trash in a ditch

Now your face has turned blue

From me strangling you

You'll never again say, "fuck you bitch"

thirst

Rick drank himself drunk to go cheat

He thought he was being discreet

After leaving the bar

He was pinned by our car

Until both halves of Rick hit the street

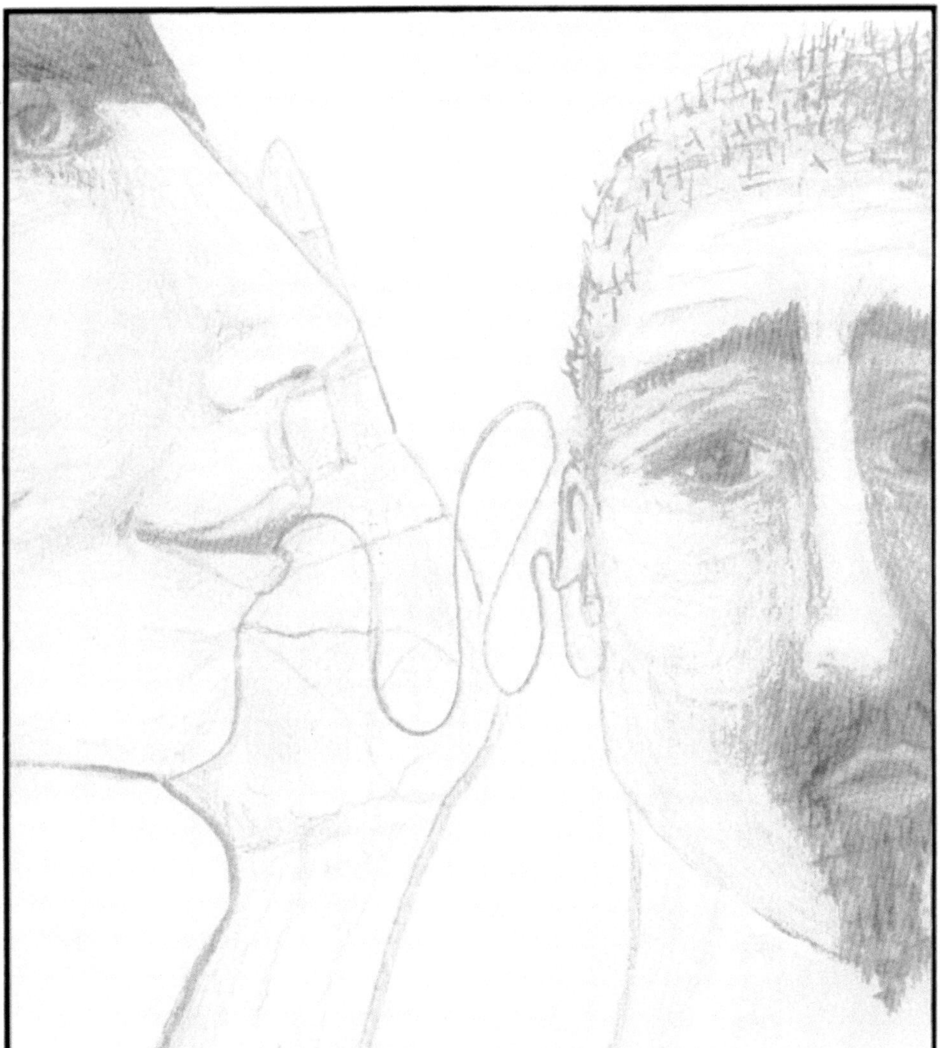

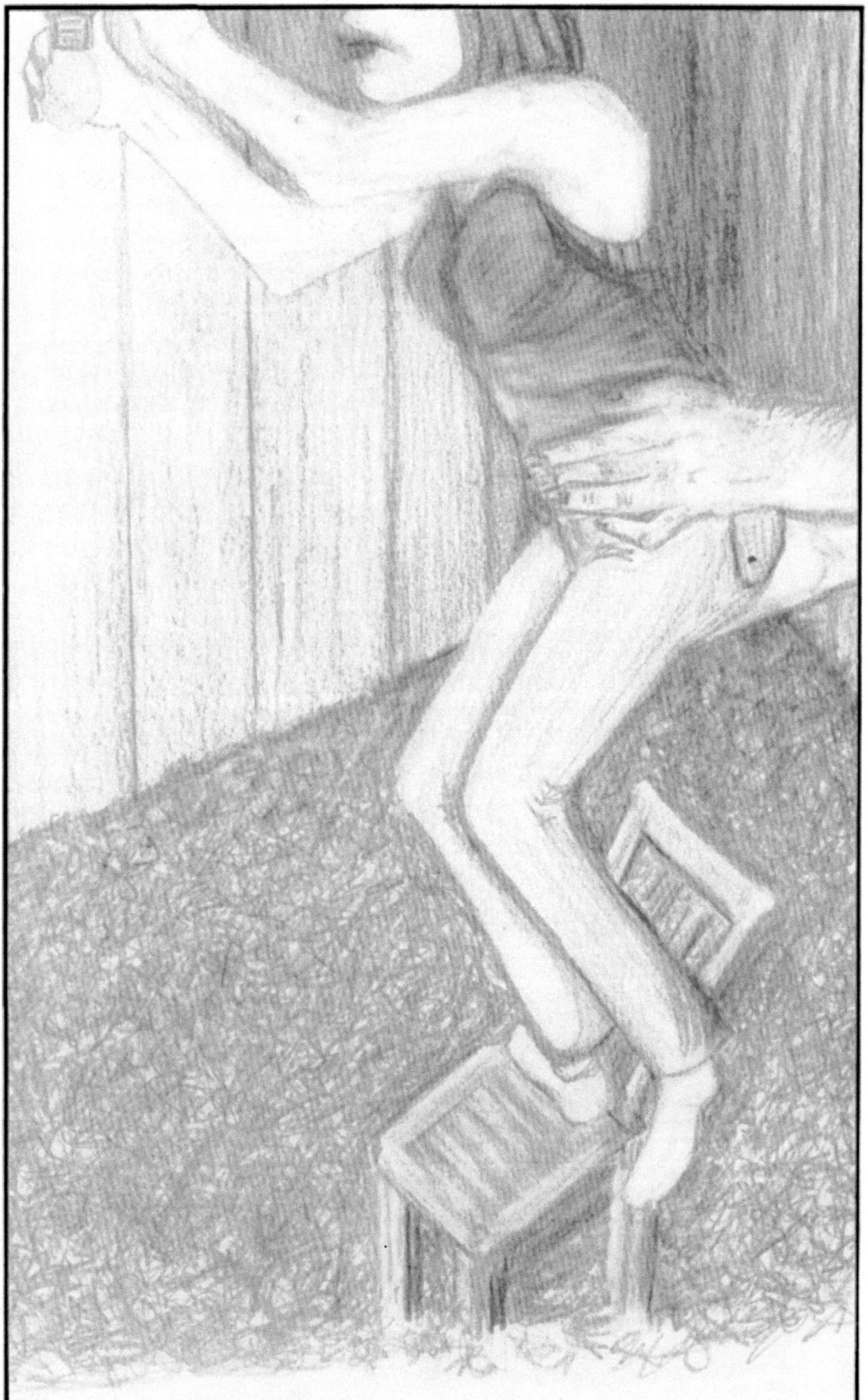

don't touch

Old Ted gave me work to house-clean

But one day he got really obscene

When I tried to run

He said, "Just having fun"

So I punched him and fled from the scene

dark

Pete forced Dan to have anal sex

Dan awaited the drugs' full effects

And knocked out in the freeze

It made his job a breeze

As his bone saw chopped Pete into specs

darker

Stef and I seemed just fine for 8 years

He left after our son died at birth

A steak knife cut his belly

His guts pouring like jelly

As he birthed out his bowels for my mirth

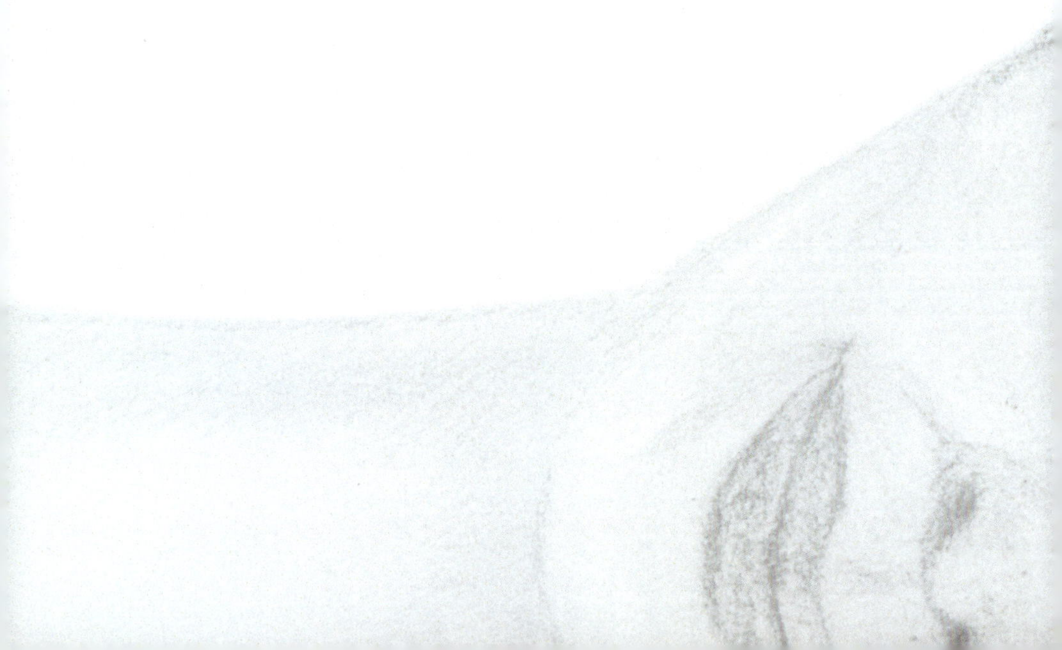

darkest

Milk still came for our son who was dead

His quick icy heart messed with my head

Cries for help went unheard

"I could stab," I concurred

Meaning jail time; some help, food, and bed

Hmmmm…

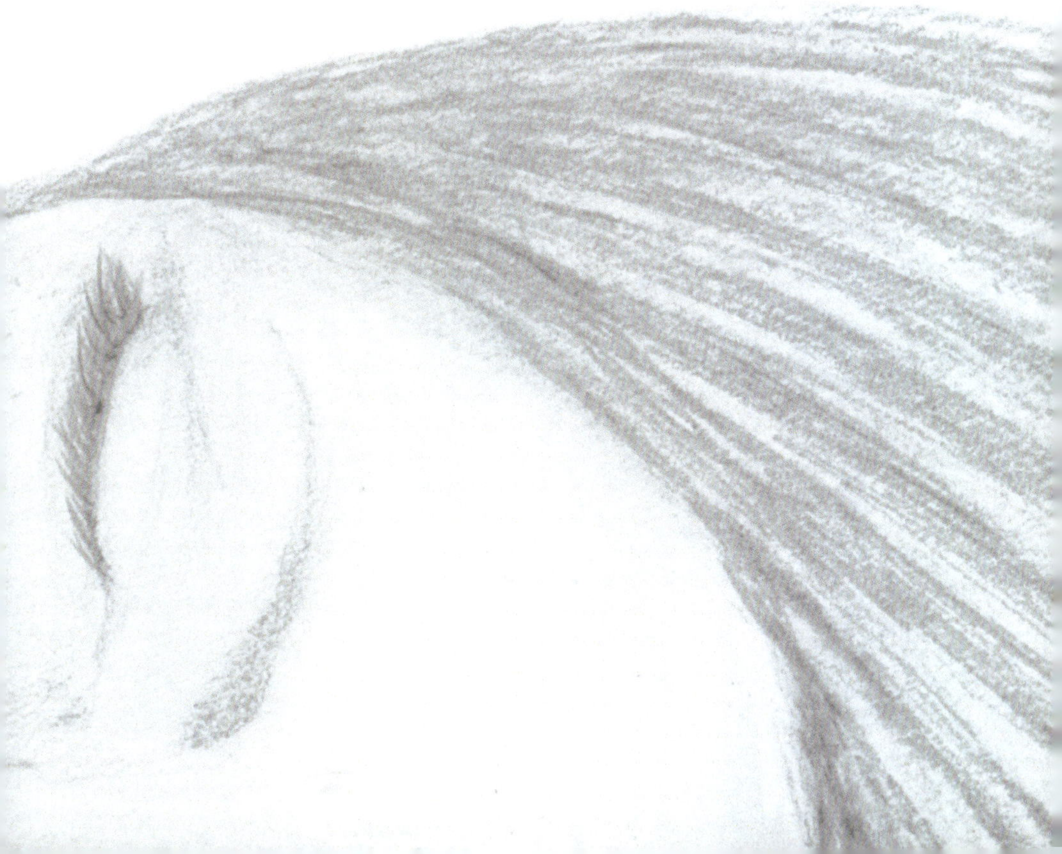

still of the night

Kent pushed me and choked me one night

Out of nowhere he held me down tight

He was shocked I suppose

When my boot smashed his nose

He didn't expect such a fight

east

In Japan I was hostess to men

I was cute and naïve way back then

A perv followed me home

Who was shining his chrome

He was found face down in an Onsen

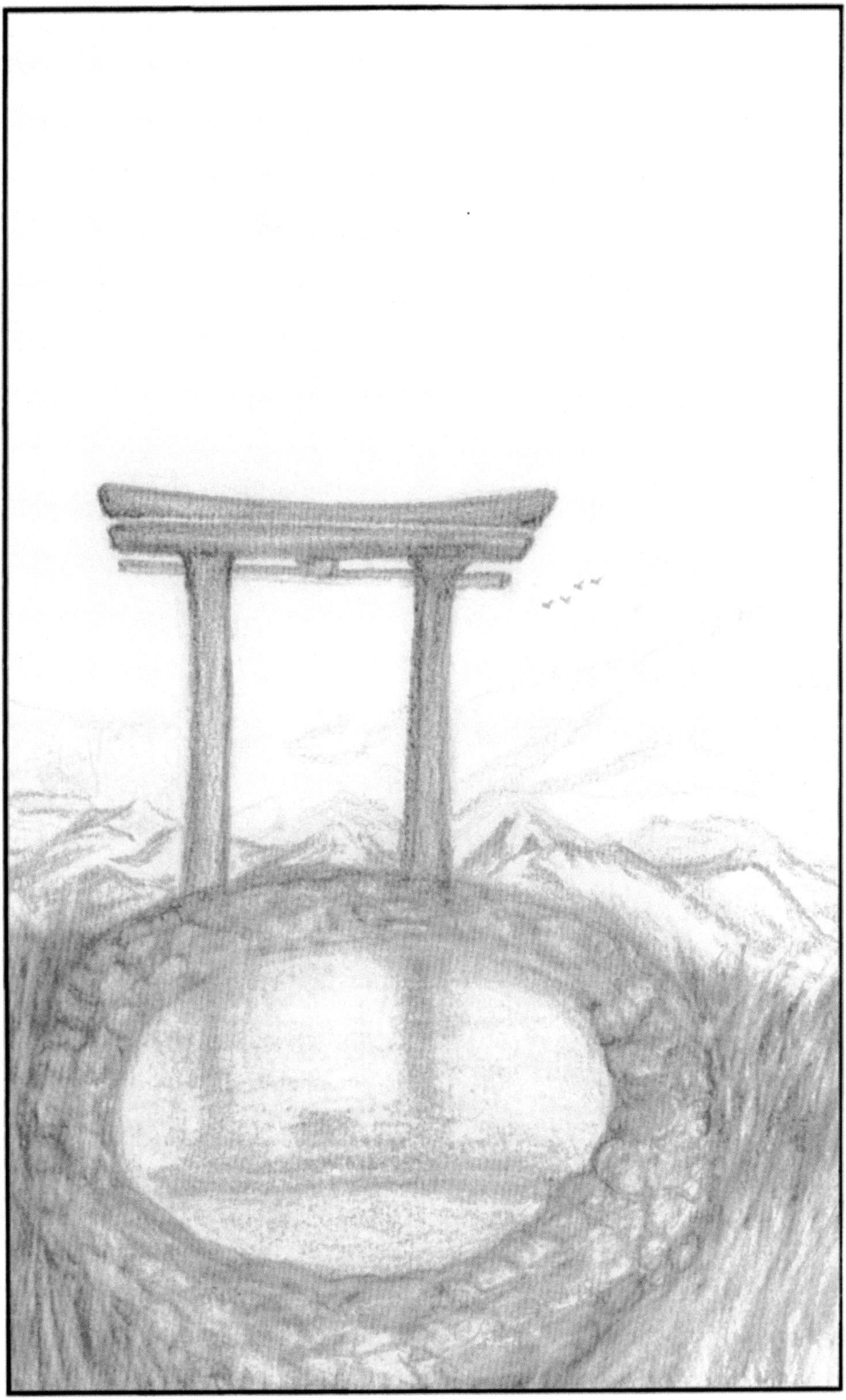

denial

Michael and Dee got along

But something with sex was just wrong

He swore he wasn't gay

'Til she caught him that way

They bled out but it took very long

out of control

She married that drunken prick Bill

Whose mood swings would give you a chill

His attitude stunk

And he often drove drunk

With no brakes he took quite a bad spill

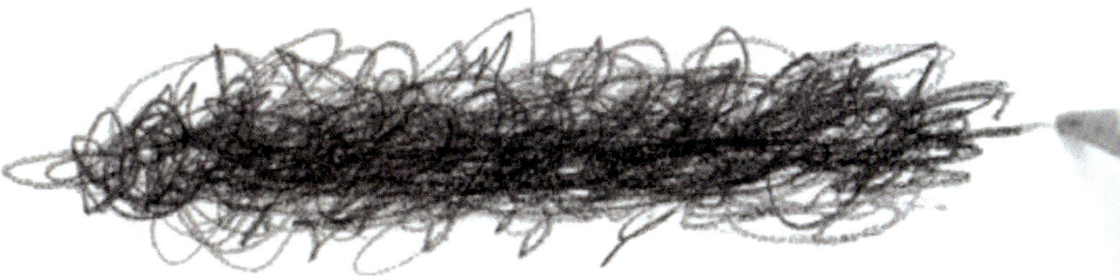

in time

Lou worked by day on the oil rigs

By night he played drums doing gigs

But Lou took off his ring

And had many a fling

So his body was fed to our pigs

beautiful friends

Why do people tell all of these lies?

Could we just have some decency guys?

If it's just sex you want

There are brothels to haunt

We're not objects to dehumanize

compulsion

Johnnie seemed like a nice man

I was really quite blind to his plans

He had online, live sex

Can you guess what came next?

My hammer smashed both of his hands

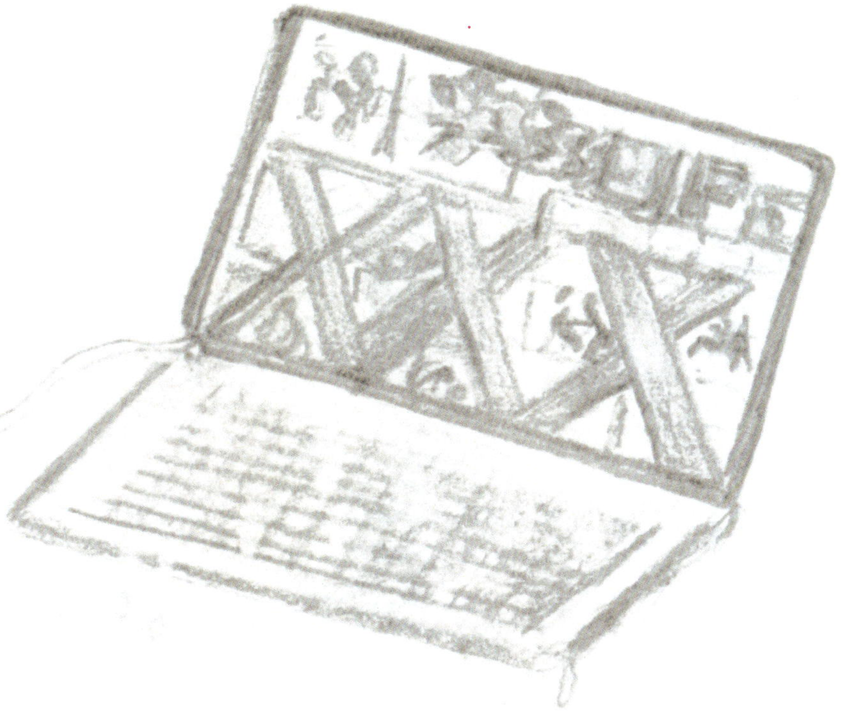

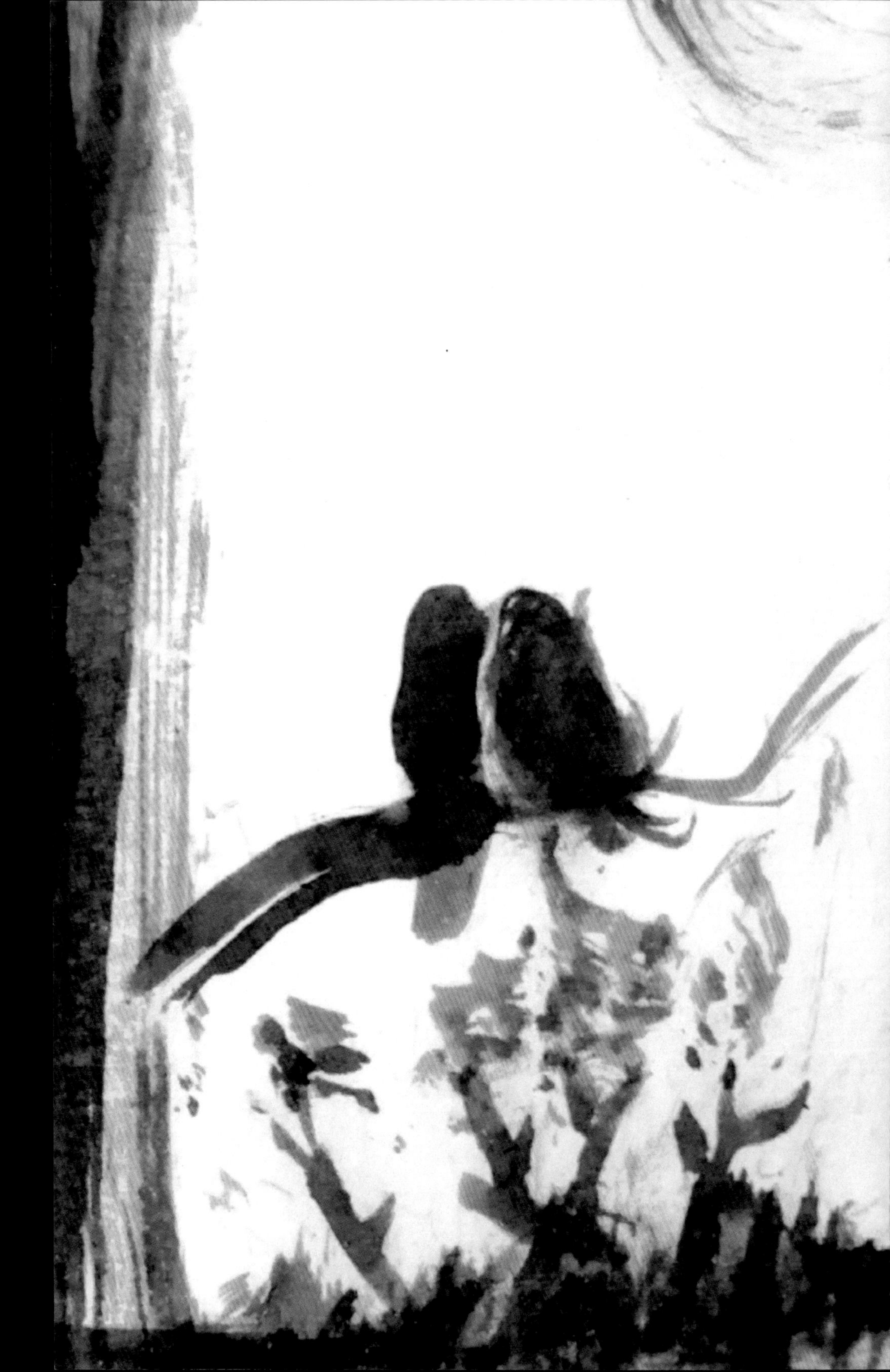

every move you make

Jerry grew up in New York

He seemed like a sweet, gentle dork

But he loved watching porn

From midnight 'til morn

So I plucked out his eyes with a fork

you belong to me

Creepy Neil filmed us girls without telling

When we caught him he just started yelling

We were sick of his tricks

So we beat him with sticks

Hematomas made him quite a swelling

pale death

George treated sweet Amy like crap

She said, "Have a bath and a nap"

Then into the drink

A hairdryer did sink

And that old bastards body got zapped

without a trace

Andrew was sexting my sister

He told me that he only kissed her

I was very discreet

And arranged them to meet

As their cabin lit up like a glister

redemption

And still more…then came fireman Fred

Those were such dirty words that he said

But he got really rough

I had bruises and stuff

And right now there's an axe in his head

Our dementia wing had a Don Juan

No one knows for how long it went on

He was found in a Gran

That despicable man

What to do with such demonic spawn?

salvation

Jodi grabbed at my breasts from behind

As a boy Jodi might've been fined

Friends first must say yes

Some risks too large to "guess"

Stealing without RESOLVE is unkind

Things make much more sense as I age

For years I held onto outrage

But I'm no longer mad

The cold always die sad

Every cold act is paid with a wage

take me home

"Why me?" cried the one who touched hate

"Why **not** me?" said the wiser of fate

Staying soft **prevents** pain

'**My** clean record's **my** claim

It's **all** that makes anyone great

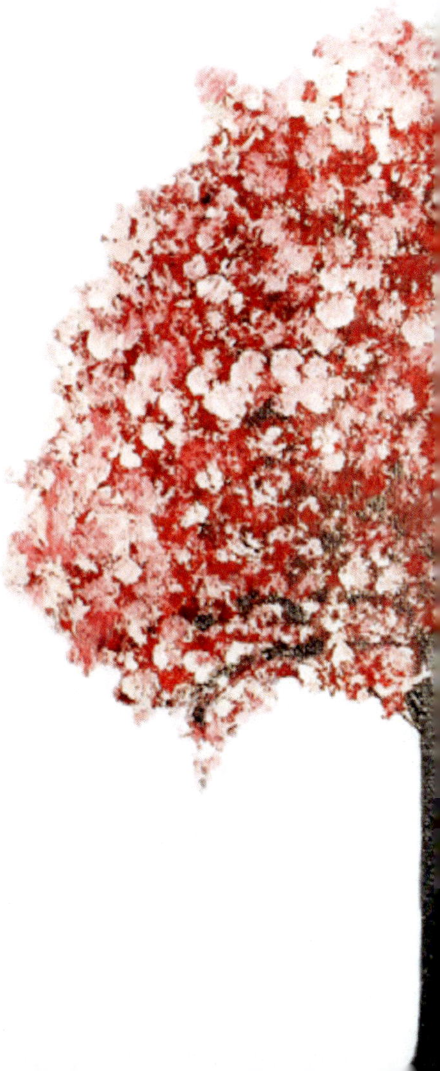

50 Ways to Bleed Your Lover

This book is dedicated
to my husband and best
friend ever, Jason Dunphy
and to all of the likewise
heroes and heroines who
have mastered the art of
human dignity despite
boyish worms.

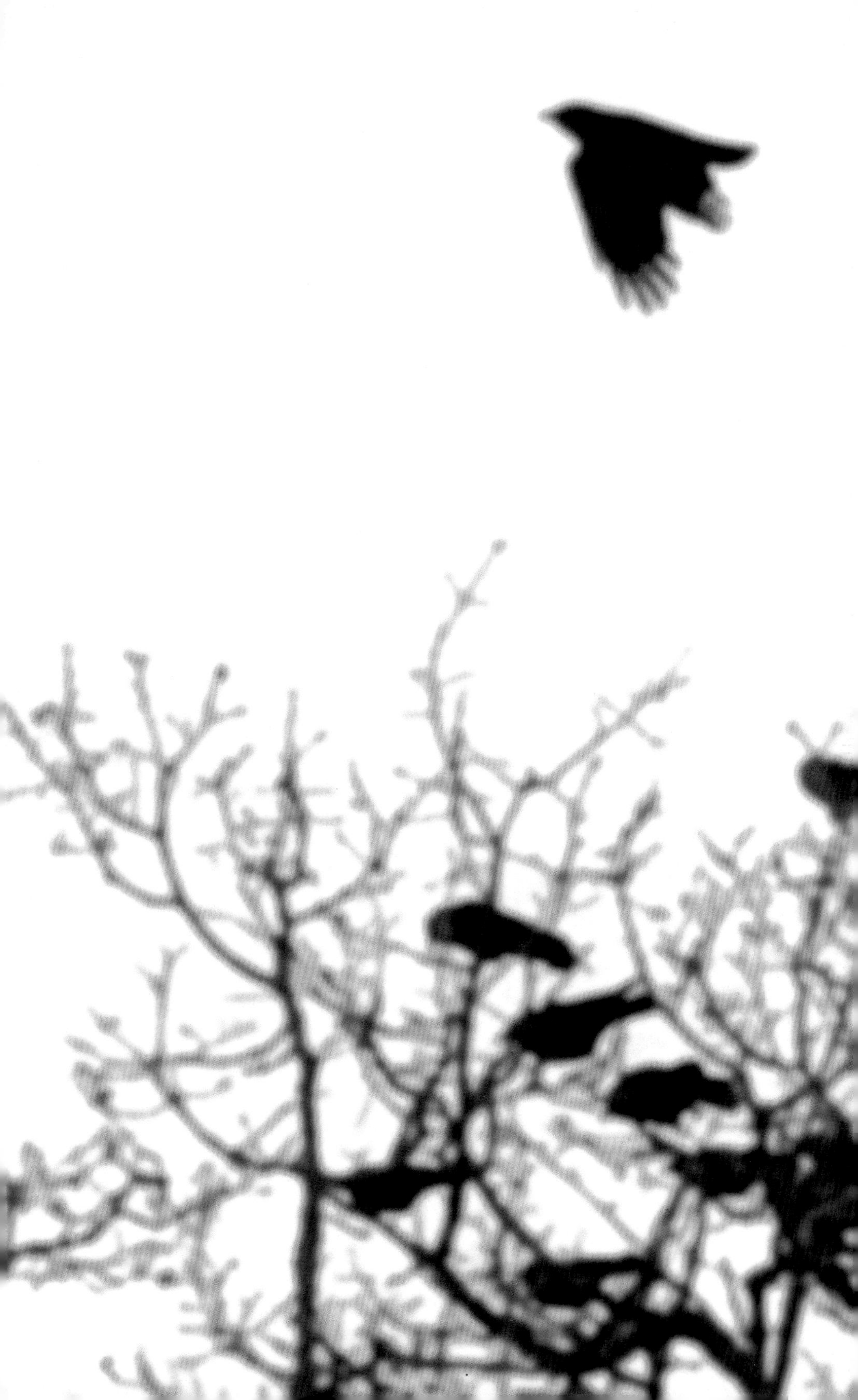

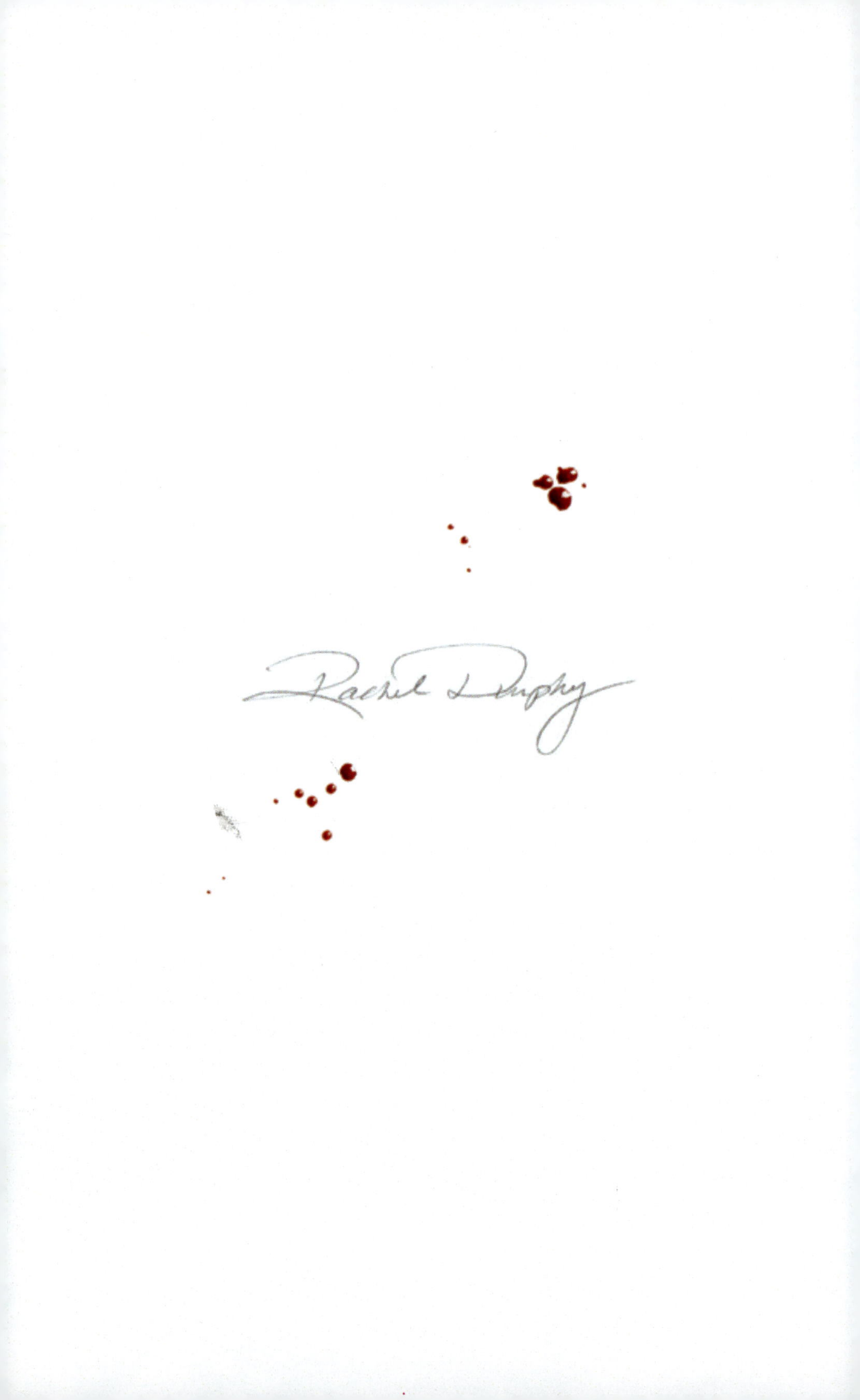